Certain Slants

for Cynthia, Kate, and Nora

Charles Alexander

Certain Slants

Junction Press

New York

2007

Library of Congress Control Number: 2006939395
ISBN: 978-1-881523-16-1
Junction Press PO Box F New York NY 10034

Earlier versions of some of these poems have been published
in the following journals and websites: *Alterran Assemblage,
Traffic, Jacket, Boxkite, Big Allis, Eoagh, Cauldron, Talisman,* and
the *Electronic Poetry Center.* Several have appeared as chap-
books: *Pushing Water 1–6* (Minneapolis: Standing Stones
Press, 1998); *Pushing Water 7,* with *Three Poems* by Tom
Raworth (Tucson: Chax Press, 1998); *Four Ninety-Eight to
Seven* (Buffalo: Meow Press, 1998); and *Aviary Corridor*
(Kenosha, Wisconsin: Light & Dust Books, Word Press, and
Chax Press, 1993). "Aviary Corridor" has been set to music
by Tim Risher. "Suspend" was choreographed by Anne
Bunker (Orts Theatre of Dance, Tucson 2000).

Contents

I

Color Field   11
Blue Does Yellow   12
Certain Slants   18
Aviary Corridor   21
Four Ninety-eight to Seven   23
Certain Shifts of Continent May Be Predicted   28

II

Pushing Water 1: *this strange man turning*   33
Pushing Water 2: *newspaper on the counter*   35
Pushing Water 3: *test scores rising to fifty per cent*   37
Cardinal 1: *as if there could be a spiral*   39
Cardinal 2: *tendency of modern law*   40
Cardinal 3: *to utter and to let*   41
Pushing Water 4: *I said in a dream the person allows to never*   42
Pushing Water 5: *fine, and wind this around until one day*   44
Cardinal 4: *angle of incident, as with*   46
Cardinal 5: *the book made to lie down in*   47
Cardinal 6: *jolting here to triangular*   48
Pushing Water 6: *a mind a terrible of linguistic changes*   49
Cardinal 7: *metaphysics of youth*   52

III

Pushing Water 7: *sea : likes   from : forgiveness*   55
Pushing Water 8: *condensation to the air of equal desire*   57
Cardinal 8: *sometimes taking the words from*   59
Cardinal 9: *this is the bouncing thing*   60
The Presence of Truth, the Present Truth   61
Cardinal 10: *You have the name right*   66
Cardinal 11: *How did you fit*   67
Dare He Hum   68

IV

Pushing Water 9: *thank you for the book*   75
Pushing Water 10: *the rose is green*   76

Pushing Water 11: *put paint on paper*   78
Pushing Water 12: *certain slants*   79
Pushing Water 13: *not the rhyme but the measure*   80
Pushing Water 14: *one sister says to the other*   81
Pushing Water 15: *some precepts*   83
Cardinal 12: *only comes into*   85
Cardinal 13: *made a line*   86
Pushing Water 16: *from the tragic foot   the variable foot*   87
Pushing Water 17: *some precepts for morning and children*   88
Pushing Water 18: *from Halfdane at Hrothgar*   90
Pushing Water 19: *she never said   my mother that is*   92
Cardinal 14: *because asked for*   94
Pushing Water 20: *the house of art has white walls*   95
Suspend   96
Pushing Water 21: *(Meryle Alexander 1918-)*   104
Cardinal 15: *will you carry a light*   107
Cardinal 16: *green*   108

V
Pushing Water 22: *a speech*   111

VI
Pushing Water 23: *for Jackson Mac Low*   123
Pushing Water 24: *for Robert Creeley*   128
Pushing Water 25: *Astrobiology as Perfume*   130
Cardinal 17: *as cost to counter —*   133
Cardinal 18: *flying Tatlin's glider*   134

VII
Pushing Water 26: *a wind blows now to then*   137
Pushing Water 27: *and only the stories we tell ourselves*   139
Pushing Water 28: *there it is   the quivering of llines*   144
Pushing Water 29: *What is the structure of a leaf?*   145
Pushing Water 30: *what two?   Watteau*   149
Pushing Water 31: *rage on across the air*   151
Cardinal 19: *jewels glow and breathe out*   152
Pushing Water 32: *polis and   politicization*   153

I

Color Field

The red amulet provides a charm against impotence, providing there is no threat. A woman called herself a witch or everyone's grandmother. Red goes out from the eyes and comes back through clouds on the horizon in the peace of sunset.

In a blue field (the words and lives) perhaps of water, what breaks the membrane of the surface? The rising and setting. The going forth and returning.

An older teacher who often wore brown suits described life as a series of leave takings. And the earth is brown in places. Attitude also changes.

There are black holes which bear weight, and it matters whether those places are absence or presence, and it's argued that black means no color, we are all colors and eventually go to black.

She picked out a new green shirt for me at a thrift shop. Green emerges in spring in lush wet climates, and goes away again. Green liquid runs in mysterious dreams; imagine a long run on a green field. Retrace your steps carefully.

A lemon's whole strength. Peel it. Turn it in your hand. Egg yellow. Return every morning and watch the boat with yellow sail come to the dock. A yellow amulet signified safe return, providing that where you are going is in question

Blue Does Yellow

pit or pitter pat and
is that, a drover
and an open door, a coo
in the corner, border
of a telling, a legend
in time, ink spilled
much gentle forest origin
corner of wood, a step
a step a step and a turn
into a green and
clear, where something is
and and string to a point

an edge and a trust, a line
to thrust to a plane
with and with a call
toward, front only only
not first or second not
only, the reward, the
reward being a told time
this was this was taken
front lends to leans to
one carrot, a stick and
a bitter bitter foraging
still a line and remind
still a line

eye glasses are guardians, to
what to what, from mine to
yours, upon a blanket and a stretch
to make a round (around are
round), clench stretch, clench
stretch, turn, formally a knee
formerly, she forms an ally
under a tree under the
under, light contains a
skin and yellow does blue,
to you remove, blue

a white room to look into
lay down down, form a
line bent, from the hip
an arm alarm, to the
south, runs into cloth
and clear edges knock
knock on the wall a
wait and tall longing
to a fall, weight rises
announce, a noun's risk
into merriment, a part
aspirate and mark a
noise and reach, a reach
for

a round and a side to side
to side, from the beginning
from the middle humming
a song a morning song
to the station alive to home
find the dog, mind the door
after a day and a night after
to please the please the
tongue, after hours amuse
the minute, prior, watch
eyes watchful

come and call occasion
corner upon square one
for toss to toss out not
out, then star on
blanket, answer with
head, eyes up follow
words across a
cross stick no
puzzle pedals round the
fold or not, forgive is
known and can't be
fiddle, fed
harmonics include a clue
led to meadow, eddy

far going field
there another room
fair room two moves
away the dark walk
a call a call calls
something listening all
ways, wait and sleep and
sleep awake, full all
follow a cry, cry in
a corner, repeat for
me, ooh or ringling
no fooling take off
circles, ring
all round, love moves
a leg or more, there

from a narrow not
upon the letter
sounded pleasure please
the measure me or
you can say gain
we know what
speaks not spoken can
answer, not question
not, move mouth
throat tight
loose let loose again
a certain treasure
mark my words mark
tongue let live
again alive

drive away and why
go why there aware so
boat rock a leaf
falls down down upon
meadow sidewalk hop
to song float low
ground again why go
so and so and so and
sound and through or
where, again you say
or did who might
upon a limb and life
risks fold not lost
when over, book and
forth it there it there it
is a strain train here
yes with her, again

making an out not
hidden, open and closed
a book page one leads
turn return a map
or place not rendered
sounded not out way
a making, fortune
desire desire is for
meaning a question
there I ask my
dare I find again
turn open closed
the water what responds
as hidden, look left
again, or eye desires

ambled led to bed
to black dog sleeps
a night sleep day
away gone child not
waiting a cry cries
a weight lost and open should
anyone ask, a stretch
stretch a turn
a look to look
here the light fades
say right of way
where holds close
sleep to shoulder hold
head upon a line
a line to there a point and

happy to breast to
move to room answer cry
why, food or dream
again from other than
other sings night
to rest upon skin
skin upon, again
to lay eyes lay eyes
upon another not
a room alone a
home two three and
everything through moves
hopeful sing to
corners and and and

Certain Slants

Opinion corners a wave.
Stairs lead to an unopened crease.
The walls had been narrowed.
A door was unnecessary.

Seeds germinate in snow.
Wrap a tune around a branch.
Key corners elicit serial motivations.
This eye requests a circus.

Strength resides in melodies.
The edges keep expanding.
To flex is to turn sweetly.
For the moment, it all depends.

Professionally bred, they bite the population.
In a rented vehicle, she read me *The Circus of Dr. Lao*.
A sign instructed rattlesnakes to exit.
We visited two hundred fourteen towns in twenty-seven days.

This moves like a stray cat.
A child runs down a street screaming with joy.
Register yours now, before the deadline.
For expansion, bite the moon.

All possible participles participate.
The play was attacked for its language.
The Manchurians prevailed and their language is dominant.
She opened the jar and waited.

Freedom rides a banana.
She goes in a blue thought she goes.
He wasn't willing to pay the cost.
The situation is fluid.

Protectionism and unilateralism form trade policy.
My father never talked a blue streak.
We pull letters from a black box.
The sky never turned a somersault.

Lists include their own undoing.
She eats a pear with two hands.
For a moment I thought you were gone.
I walks, he walks, they underestimate.

At the movie she met a stranger.
Take the twelve-thirty flight, it's less prepared.
It tests one's ability to manipulate concepts.
Information is overrated.

A gift comes unannounced, unconcerned.
Lack of profit was not a factor in its demise.
Mariachis surprised us at noon at the café.
After a fashion, it comes to a close.

A journalist and an architect were separated by an interval.
A person described as a mathematical function.
Stay close, she will need you.
The color is the film's fault.

Inside a frame she loses her buoyancy.
Public policy retreats in a periplum.
For instance, you twist your hair
Curled lips impart a fine-tuned sensuality.

They understood, and were forgiven.
Jury duty calls upon an ability to reason according to custom.
Imagination is not required.
Sleep is underrated and overdetermined.

It moves toward overstatement.
Redundancy isn't possible.
Newspaper oversights produce assonance.
The key to the flight was a sense of balance.

She, a nurse, goes to the gulf.
Cerebral operations are military chic.
We walk on a cold evening looking at lights.
A cry stifles a cry.

She traded a painting for a fireplace.
Shades of green and blue.
He dreams *kalapuya* and phones not often.
He lives alone upstairs and I miss him.

The paint in the kitchen looked like pepto bismal.
Let rise for twenty minutes in the pans, she forgot.
She remembered to alter the exterior.
Fright reminds, repairs, pretends.

Consider, she thought, the rejoinder.
The laser's heat is considerable.
Someone primed the engine.
Doubt proliferates.

Receive a bonus with each entry.
Her delight was audible, muscular.
The tone darkened.
They sat three to a table.

Aviary Corridor

After an outdoor installation by Cynthia Miller at the Tucson Botanical Gardens

I.   hallelujah chorus

swift fusion

the agony of worship

beneath a tree

not the world

in a green coat

2.   aviary corridor

hummingbirds fly through red hoops

a bit of wood

remembers

the markings

stemmed tides

3.   a night's lodging

who is watching

twice willing

4.   garden for girders

underpass mural

5.   I know a man

who said that

6.   a bowl of soup

watch the thermometer

around a river

runs, alters, something

7.   she becomes

the only

music

8.   frayed at the edges

figs, branches

Four Ninety Eight to Seven

When asked, at age three, "What time is it?," Kate
Alexander replied, "four ninety eight to seven."

small white chair in a painting

for nine, tea
ate toes, even
valleys between whole numbers

commingling with leaves

prayer in the shape of
bread, sticks
in the mood

seductive arms, leaning, bending

a lovely lingering lane
stretch to toe to heel to touch
a light an eye an ovule

presence not symbol

where an over from
pear form a deer throw toward
never that tree again

nonsense, pageantry

new year soft
turnaround turnaround
and very pressed against a wall

blue bricks interlaid in a wall

Santa Monica boy
bowling alley beignet café
wanderer

three dogs and a red-haired doll

laughing
or
not

clay heart, worn well

thought turning to
leaf in the
prescribed wilderness

twentieth breath, not counting

honey bear honey
bee honey
comb   unkempt

this impression, not well inked

to say the state
clear and
glistens snowbound

an accent, interposed

when given a choice of *yes*
or   *no*   choose
or

no such particle as a fragment

seven and eight
numbers tempt
and question faith

attention span junkie

enlightenment bones
or a state of un-
measured wind

life of the cowboy mesa heart

complete thought
of (im)possible
x's and o's

arrow through spine, a crease

trajectories pose
a weight
blintzes for breakfast

squared, grid lines hardened

same clothes
two days, shame
an odor

a chart   a trace

or laugh
when not
else any works

assumption of powers, dreamer

the following day
the following day
the following day

subtle sex   a rumble

a promise
can be a sigh
sight   to see

vowel sliding to vowel, coercive aorta

a sigh to C
the keyboard beckons
awry

calling a friend, a digital act

not green enough
follow yearning
folded along a line

did see a forest, facing east

paper
stitched and folded
repeated tasks

twenty two a number counting

fine mist breath
imagined spark   real
wires and sockets

shooting this way and that, frills and most fine

light travels
light again
travels again

accounting for taste

plate full, exotic
food
ample thigh

absorption, blue, radial

and more
white space
and

small white chair in a painting

Certain Shifts of Continent May Be Predicted

Apostles' flowing accommodations, robes for the pilgrims
showing signs of wear, sing only arias, can it
summon meetings of unequal duration, as in
caesura heading for the cliff's edge, walk toward angels
only when dust and drawings remember a friend,
without crayons or sarcasm, he needed one, perhaps four
and only found meditation possible with toxicity, strange
books made of pencils and torn pages, not enough
time to announce the inevitable, going through madness
or laughing, sometimes the path does not diverge to
garden, frost only at higher altitudes where for days
there have been no clouds, remembered haiku the rim
of what human lingers where before, himself

Strange the motion of weather, unending dry
and fault to a premium, assurance of text falters
hair to hand, oil stick and false witness bars entry,
no hand to breast, or either wish to carousel,
a walk to winter from a landscape of pipestone's
washed surface, ice breaking now on missed island's frame
of referring one to three, take two places away from the master,
directing boards to state the obvious, mispronounced
with insult, stand at the podium and treat the microphone with ease
because nothing talks, no one sat in assembled chairs without ears
folded and gone home, though flowers remain from a year gone,
other's accented space with orange cries, no rushes
in water, nothing filtered through gaps in the stitching

Strong breathing chokes the independent rise from
pushing wanting the air to furnish identical gaps in knowledge,
fashion rings as upsets rule a game in transition, always
forgetting what came before among, stem making room for
leaves, plant this in your pot of framed sensibles, two means
separating red from green and blue, absolving
vision from the living room conversation, when that
doesn't work touch the hip with no cloth, no fault for opening
door to rain in a storm, pray for it, shift all the books
until there is no exit possible without taking
someone with another idea entirely, faithful
even when silent dining makes for families at war
with the borders of relation, fanfare for the starving

Buckets and moments of storm's decay meaning sun
posed for eyes concerned with protect or weather from
family merging, wanting lack of noise, farms if
never a part of fortune wanders unpaved, only in
western Oklahoma has the cotton dried beyond
itself, thread of a book's signature in folding dethroned
from prayer, mounted firm on board, gray
cloth as in winter, there again the storm extends
nearly to April, the eyes focused to sew precisely
each section, don't for moments crease wave or flay
extravagant arms on subsequent body, layer and edge
of asking, what words say there no speak not left to
chance digress, after close or else, where go

II

Pushing Water 1

        this man strange turning
                forgetful though not in a line
abiding to want oranges not a color so much as
            through the tunnel pushing water
               reading a turn into some blue note
       ashes brass gate closed but a space under
          level or tool for moving
       same but shadows on
          brown boxes, books, yellow cat
nothing lists as if breathing matters, crocus
   beside, along, otherwise aslant
      and stripes, sure, can't away now or want
        doing for reach, elbow still

       surprises unfurnished, as though
leaving means line break, body
             open, callous, asking without rancor
        not what keeps
   night's premise that points never starry
             say what one wall, hearing owls among
rising a single point for
        horizon's will, my or their intention
   witnessed, ever, walking for
    notions, encounters, as fine this hour
     a line wants edge, aloof and
         strengthened with no idea
ground upon lack turning other to cheeks' sadness
        ripe, lively wanting or unstraightened
    enough to place in mouth, hand, wash
       taste down forks upon nothing
  accordingly, original upheaval merges rimless
engraved with Defoe's initials plunging sea-like
    concerned with the address of a rose
       (static wanders to empty spaces)
    suits or untied hair muted
  a long time ago a trumpet g-sharp to b, odd sonority

unfounded with an oboe, *pierrot,* re-beckoning
the border is not necessarily a margin
that gap water permeates / asking
hosannas to be silent / prayer may be received or taken
while sitting, facing wood, politics closed to mourners
another world jumps on fathers / some paragraphs
announcements and justice poses a fable
prayer and the book try to make responsible
deaf or out from under / that space the subsequent (previous)
appearance of children, imperatives, request
the occupation of bare feet, high sounding
in open territory or aware

Pushing Water 2

newspaper on the counter
strikes a chord, stem attached
can't recommend a board or
stain in cement from that public disunion
erupting in black white lettered squares
on tops of tables around the bend masking
where tenacity wins a day's approval brooding
before no stars   /   are you tracing
a line of exit, assuming
whenever money flees to prearranged adoption tears
several times in two days, arithmetic
words defined in acknowledgement, fire tuned within
stories, transition and imported free of custom
writing as of reverse, form winged and baseless
believed she in angels and painted small numbers
white marks on black until drained, small
man with heart for head, literally
undone by fumes, horizons wanting place to breathe
savagely uttered fine droppings stain
to free basil humbly offers no pity
arc and foundational, light
as substance   /   he never knew what that meant

actual green wall and cat drawing near music
as if batteries matter
previewed to mass arching
wrapper hinged between two or more alternatives
materials infected   /   daily dispersion
and lack of candles telling children to sleep
too long for attention reading scrawls
from oak, alder, politic picking plum
to aphasia   /   render problem graphically
as bassoon under meadow grass rolling with her
bravo show a hit
where humor frames until
space deplanes declares abruptly

crumbled intelligence into back yards string determines
theory of presence, prayer
a far rattle reaching solvent fray torrent soil
black to stand asking no fault
no red at all, still

Pushing Water 3

test scores rising to fifty per cent a balancing act
        wide gap between free lunch and full pay
    afraid of retension   (*fan shen* / a village turns over)
                a culture flags its children
        and shares a bone moment of prayer
      pain killers at hand seven days
              and a bus ride to possible
        extinction no past in sight
           in snow bound bundles
      arguing budget lines through the wind   /   stability
             or sustenance enchant
      ties and laces underneath tables
             through the frost
        arrows pushing parts as final, mouth
           utters small noise
    from legs the time barters to state unless
yes please give me a call irises with riverbed names rise
        into cloud cover, aurora regrets not
    strains in cotton from an altitude frightened
           children in closets
    as national debt comes to equal executive compensation
afraid of children shouting at 3 a.m.
         a two year old who says /
     the yellow's gone
            there are pastures and horses
   somewhere in northern Oklahoma riding four hours
   whole
    ambidextrous only in baseball's green hat with A for a name
untended, unturned, unflappable, unscrewed,
       wide eyed long in the nose
       He told a story of loss
  but listening strayed to boxes resembling hay on the prairie
    my uncle bundled when I knew where I lived where
there's
     an I know that /   no talent for riddles the first
      person excised from will to burn / it did

happen it   happen will   happen arrogant

to a fall from grace
push to pay for prayer in a needlecap   /   tip
dripping unlike
smearing or knots in lace
when found as an arrow drew curtain reft road
buried in snow today the
girls made snow bunnies less than a week pre Easter
crisp
memory, nor crisp nor stale just broken, rose to
sky's pale gray for occasional porter
where no green makes knowledge under the table
with your leg between straws
prior to aching the whole of joy as utterance
tossed to play at some cost, indented
semblance come to
another's desire and walking around a block
with serendipitous leveling nothing
awkward the rain night's charm and apt
to love speech or keeping faith
within age rock and carving spires above eye level

Cardinal 1

as if there could be a spiral
        forget nomenclature upon
        a rock or water
  aspirant, sensible
        practicing no more than
        three metaphors — including
        at least one in which
        an imagined family
        structure figures prominently
can weeds grow in red rock?
C: a letter with no *inside*
inside a mind which is
four years old and without
conventional language
                sibilant, flying
        questioning the legal extremity
        to a point so heavily
        metaphoric that oil
        matters less than
        witness

Cardinal 2

tendency of modern law
  created without rock and
  its attendant flaw, line
  leading to person, order
  imposed by escape from
  criticism, violent critique
  of character and the state
before you know the bodies
               wash hands
       as one never predicts
       luster or outcome
more numerous homes in
the basin, arrived at
a plus or minus room,
one where foreign relations
achieve no stasis
       crying for three
       quick movements
       bodies a stranger sees
       acquainted and done

Cardinal 3

to utter and to let
   the person in, proper
   burial and the limit
   of passion, absence
   of nothing, there goes
         the cursor, articulate
         light —
tell me of the social,
where it begins and ends,
against the moving point
                please wash before
                entering room or
                field, permission
                to dispense with
                prayer
         came asking, rate of
         response, number of
         pleasures standing
         in a line, dialogue
         with color

Pushing Water 4

I said in a dream the person allows to never
begin with an I, rim after rain unsteady,
could waltz or polka to chicken scratch from San Xavier
saints moving with a hot wind and now the canyon waters
frighten birds into aeries and out again
can reversal win the day, the colloquial
uncertainty, as always
one is solid and usually startled to find imagination
as in dreams of Johnson, Shakespeare, Eliot
and Pound that fascism a constant argument, and one
of mountains, Tarahumara, this body aches
to run and aches when running, and after,
OK we can come together now, again
your chest against mind, was it hot wind or
a blue pool in a painting, archeology
as deconstructed as mass against density free of
totalitarian construct saving grace for tomorrow
jealous off stage when nothing arrives despite aspirations, echo
saving blue pen for glide or hesitation into orgasm
grain in wood captures meander as if sticks frame the picture
of laceration, ashes, fortune
and a fiddle, harmonica mother's instrument of choice, a
slap on the knee and sharply to mouth the notes neither
hesitant nor true, sister's kick in the back
one of four memories of pain, mostly moving from home
to country or state
as in Hawaii, Oklahoma, Texas, Japan, Missouri, straw, pitchfork,
watermelon, struck knee night missed turning road washed
to sky's mirror, lost in auto
aforementioned string music, *solfege's* lost opportunity
asking for books in winter, advantage of incompletion
flocks of blue styled in loose garment,   grasping
as if no place or activity takes root
from another's fear, five amid field green
what passed between   /   phrases or aphasia
names of alleged survivors
you follow, thick between wind in anything exposed to

intended consequences, balance on moon terra cotta plastic
from glass blown by movement southeast to northwest
even though all remains within six hours of the western ocean
historical place of the book
where even a prayer lifts from the page
alternative to frog plop, away
from entry, pages are kind to fingers, memory
as if spoken   /   letters gathered in a field
high scanning density   /   technical matter leading to vision
holding rock from a stream as though time makes
different partners of days
vessels dead there, produced in a mill among
sounds of rustling   /   open
or unvoiced fricatives   /   tremble of after
when *mouth to* scream of *will not*
submit or force any color to that letter's print on a sheet
connection refused on the basis of standing precedes a phrase
sewn in the center tied outside the frame of reading
there a hole through escapes meditation
as three holes divide space
in a person near to knowing paper as air
and breathing   exit   fertile

Pushing Water 5

fine, and wind this around until one day you don't
anticipate a break in utterance   fanning out almost
1600 miles driving with a dog in the car
        places seen many times on such trips but not anticipated
as age defines space
                wrinkles witness experience where memory
                        plays with children and mercy
                find something to drink, please
the skin not bitter
midwest winter walking to a bus stop
                rather an ongoing gradual drain of
        moisture
the desert's long lines I didn't believe when Mei-mei talked
        reconsidered

                as in
                little mountain
                picking up
                rocks with
                two
                children

        uncertain as the force of legs almost forgotten
            but not to introduce tones of nostalgia, sex's recalcitrance
                except at the mention of mouth from land to
language

eye line
to something
beyond perhaps distance
though everything respected denies such, writes such, obliterates
        there, I said it, I think, a refusal of autobiographical purging
            or stick with the facts, rocks and dirt, xeriscaping fondly
a writing unshaped by the folding of pages, the place of ink bounded
by convention even when
each step seems the invention of form dear steven, there is something
new under the sun, but where are you

to see it with me now that I have been in houses on your street, never
forging us without a visual memory
           of some sketch you made, entrusted
to someone's care, my children miss you even as you roll
and I'd like to acknowledge certain people whose names are kept
until you return to a place it is difficult to imagine all the people you
           know who
                            you forget you know
           that underlying urgency
on a bed in a stone tower with a misspelling of *buenos dias* to become
                buenos dios, moon
                            an aging grasp of sexual release
           part of memory or otherwise only a line
           a mile a stem an iris a garden a corridor a tile
avalanche or freefall, this is where we live
                            light carpet, dark tile, green bathroom and
      a mountain range to name a daughter for
      OK so

it's all lighter than the air before
even so
un   certain   and forgetting
           pardon the personality
           I'm only considering
           retirement in the abstract
           fondling someone in a valley (or dream) (or memory)

despite systematic derangement of the social fabric of the
neighborhood   in which a child came after first emerging from
blue light in a hospital

is this clear to anyone?
and if the weather changes
                            may even ask for a seat under a painting
                            with books unloading in the basement
      arc of unsilence
      not abstention

Cardinal 4

angle of incident, as with
  a visit, two to four
  with no photographs
           finds a four bedroom
           enclosure, angels
      as though what really ensues
      is a mapping toward
      light, when instruments fail
these are words of piety
summoned, asked for
  a glass of water
  and a hand
           flung widely to
           predict the future
           with fish
  pressurized lines
  indicated by medical
  instrumentation
  a sketch, a poem, a memory
pursuing what architecture or
lack of pain recommends

Cardinal 5

the book made to lie down in
has large to be not
        encumbered
but a binding, executed
with hands
        has no pages looking
        for deliverance
never closed despite
  appearances from behind
  spine indicating
  strength and once wet
  or pierced
these are the bodies we
call our own
     having found a way through
     what light brings to
     the eye
     constructed asleep
     in a room
     weightless

Cardinal 6

jolting here to triangular
hand drawn other
space in golden
  hue or recompense
          to make a home
          added on to
          domesticity contrasts
with the nomad, although
moving now seems
possible at each point
or pointed dispersal
of person
          there light crawls
          to be loosed
  aging memories of horizon
  in the world, run down hill
  and fall into a hold
  because nothing can stop it
          mythic face triumphs
          after all and a spot
          of tea, coming home

Pushing Water 6

a mind a terrible of linguistic changes thing to minister as caroling,
　　　　wondering
what juxtapositions rejoice over hostages, dolls which eat the hair of
　　　　children or

even a clear stream of epithets, hurled
　　　　unexpectedly at men and women
　　　　　　　　on the street

stirring, making a perfect froth

day year's new on quiet is all

　　　　　　　　twelve all in a row, little, or nine, in lines
　　　　　　　　fine and among time sow, yes, grow up or
　　　　　　　　out, an amaryllis grows mostly up,
　　　　　　　　reveling in a corner window's sunlight
　　　　　　　　close to where water runs, and stuns us in
　　　　　　　　our pajamas on a Wednesday, eating bananas
　　　　　　　　with young girls, two in no row, neither a line

prying as fashion, shore up the boats for the water is coming from the
sky as a single frozen mass, needing us less than we have read in star
columns, laughing at the consistency with which time is poorly
registered, inclusive of religious health in new countries, at least in the
year of our fine tuning

q　op　ringin fo rais　stan 'o pop outla pers　　str　fr
mis　　pl　　inte　　sch　　ast　ul　　as　　transl

there's a fabric
of loss and gain

　　　　　　asterisks be damned

and can one do this without accumulation of snow
in the months of November through April

                    ?

                                   linguistic as a means of coercion
forever microphone as recipient of news about one's shoes
          they're dead, save us all from the rumble
when a line plunges cleanly into a circle, fully defining an active
landscape as the letter Q
which may occur in the seventeenth position but has never questioned
                    its own role as primary
                    local and inquisitive
                    married or simply under suspicion
                    for the contents of the soup
                    (here, too, simply a recipe with lemon)
                              acting with held tongue, that too a dance

I never suspected it would be like this
   where "I" and "it" and "this" have become elements in a cast of
hundreds
                    or at least twenty-three
and the music
is a matter
of endurance
rather than
sibilants and concussion
freedom of choice
                              is another haven
oh mythology please fail me now
poaching the badger and the hare   singing the high passage
catching the bird in the air and returning it
                              with only a hint of plucking

          we have telephoned seven times regarding the plumbing
                    and twice someone has come to look at it

50

and still there's a hole

with open air if not for a stuffing of newspaper

singing the high passage

Cardinal 7

metaphysics of youth
    fight against someone, masked
    either way it's relief hidden
    and not returned (the last word)
                responding
    an unstable language, buildings
innocent she knew the ones
extremity extremity extremity
    break the pattern of
    quotation here where
    the heart
as procedure with tensions
assert to be true, not under
oath or oats to the hungry
        assail mirth
    while occupants of a
        certain optimism
rhymed for the sensory order
  the words of Heraclitus : in
  sleep we see sleep
        perchance
            a hitherto institution
    whose task to grasp

Pushing Water 7

sea : likes   from : forgiveness

> a plum in a pocket waiting for moon to speak in eclipse as
> this night the comet attracting human attention, eye set
> on point until focus collapses a blue ring around, fencing
> sense in or entrance out — it couldn't happen on a finer
> night, visiting from Washington visiting from San Diego
> visiting from Saskatoon this is a place about visiting,
> about which visiting forms a concept in part because of
> the night sky and a level of attention which perhaps
> requires *being away from* — a kind of paying attention
> when the rose springs a rose and lack of silence replaces
> lack — I forget myself here, as we say, longing

stem : torso
mind : clarinet

asters in the morning on a silver tray or made to look like
rain, aspirate a spiral sound asking if sound has shape —
only four or five basic choices hold the mind, when
playing a concerto in the summer of 1975 did she know
each note or only approach them in groups as they
advanced, no militarism in the sense of canons forming,
only a margin from which a strategy emerges not in
response or opposition but on the side like potatoes or
melons

glass : around

at : bread

> Ask which book to choose, one takes a gray and one a
> blue and red, two a yellow ochre and there is no green

ten : ask

often　：　askance

　　　　　germane　：　enabled

beside, along, otherwise dimensionless, as if grazing on
wheat, walking there as golden winds matter a memory,
weather confronting emergence, witness this — the issue
twists to take us out of nature, become watchers in the
midwestern conception of time as a waiting place, in the
case of a true story

　　　　onion　：　leap
　　　　Derived from six sentences >

I came here tonight to interrupt sleep and watch you, hands at
　　　　　　attention, erect.
　　　Put something in my pocket.
　　　Flowers and food categorize the light.
　　　She bought books but not the gray one.
　　　One summer she was invited to play a concerto.
　　　I was having trouble with the title.

　　　　　Innocence　：　better

　　　　strum formed a boundary, as if sound could turn
　　　　one's head physically, in another direction, or so.
　　　　A small dog could as well, knowing one, chewing
　　　　a phone cord and a garden hose, things concerned
　　　　with flow, course of affection.

　　which　：　believe

Pushing Water 8

condensation to the air of equal desire   /   apparent if not stiff

as me

as if

as wanting

let the duration contend   act : alter

        the colon performs separation, conjunction, visual

        displacement, taking place, burden of place or

        brazen   bother

        never a time of not listening

        one utters   utters one

    with appended arm

waterweed in the lake, smells long summer

more plausible than the association of language

        with power over symbols

             multiple hens and eggs

                (the resurrective time of year)

      his vocal equipment, imagine the perversity of machine song

            feeding lunch to children

                who wear green dresses

                    and a look of kind

                confusion, possible language

        its inner restraints

deposit of righteousness here, tendentiousness

        along the side of the implied wall

      beam of support with pink box attached

      perhaps a message inside its door

          come upon me

      when the poet has died, we shall all come chanting sutras

           or with words on our faces, desiring

nothing but sustain   /   in place   /

        as something swings in the back yard

and a wall that has not yet been built or marked upon

imagines itself as straw gathered for charitable causes

crying the lunar
            the lair
              the air

Cardinal 8

sometimes taking the words from
books laid out on a green
table with a blue edge
in a room with 30 chairs,
a fiberglass deer
        (which now looks this way)
and, visible from this chair,
five paintings of children
        there the light
        forms an opening
        birds and wings
        go through
on their way
        the books sent from
        places of order,
        imagined tables
someone wrote a letter
and it was never received
                so how can
                we know
                the alphabet

Cardinal 9

this is the bouncing thing
    asterisks can't encompass
— not to understand
    can be a point in
    space or of departure —
admit that the ledger
        inconsequential as it may
        provide an organ
            between rain storm
            and bowling alley
and a house which sits
between a waterfall
    and an urban lake
        (this is the bouncing thing)
understand, coals don't always
flame up and make warm
        their dark and cold eyes
can be utterly deceiving
        when the water breaks
it takes time to heal
            but light suffices
            in a space
            less confined

The Presence of Truth, the Present Truth

the whole craft consists
of this winnowing

the myth politely
says goodbye

come to light or
some other matter

the basis of knowledge meaning
what doesn't go away

the clear sight line
purveyed without blinking

sentence pronouncing on
itself, depraved success

in the content and not just in the
subject and to know the difference

a laugh can just as easily
turn on you

struggle to free himself
from himself, its richness

like chattering monkeys branch
to branch, winded at last

all the attractions and repulsions
united in marriage

the last shred of belief shredded
into belief's last shred

the myth of identity's dispersion
that too, dispersed

as with silence a mode
of incomprehension

may very well be what
cannot be except in expulsion

the absence of a specific imperative
as yesterday, a mountain hike in sand

latitude and longitude
predicate in position only

phenomenon of binding without
the least bit of stitching

the age participating
in love and related matters

whatever the question that answers
the question's statement, not that

a fine aspic, knowing how it
might be constructed

whether or not
the vegetables groan

according to this sort of thinking
in fact, it is of no importance

a listing in writing of the presidents
so that one might dispense with them

but they avoid this, and can't
make light of its landing

narrative within the narrative
is it not bliss?

that frame where nothing persists
and dust does not gather

curious children are watering plants
in the small garden by the gate

the wish to sing is just a cover-up when something
outside the middle frame begins to emerge

goodbye, vaquero, in the orange hat
under the blue moon

where a sister writes a letter, writes
letters, there, on the paper, writing

lest she know
that we forget what we let her know

still point at which music turns around
music turns us around still

chronic meditations on topics meant
to come to an end, but can't

to create a curve take straight
lines and bend them, point to point

fashion heaps scorn, late on the
pinnacle of fame, strong, forlorn

hope dawned, legitimacy claimed,
judgment matured, what never knew

to set reason at variance with itself
there's a rub of thyme

my judgments are intuitions
and others' as well, until

the world at odds with the words, they
too find a way of moving toward sand

and seventeen minutes of dance in Paris
is hardly enough

the mathematical total that equals world
beyond what steps we take

the comic cosmic mortal debt
beyond what steps we take

can or can't say, proof leads to arrival,
illusory conviction, better to dream if wanting

arms rising above head, out of water, pain
where the sinews have loosened

the world is given, false the infinite, false
the limited, false the conclusion one way, or both

these are the evident self truths we find under
the bridge, away from the equal thunder, asking

we deny what we affirm we deny and we say
little or nothing in brief song, but sing less than we might

each step taken in a run makes a thousand
muscles collapse

my reader who is kind and patient knows
this year and century will not close the present

Cardinal 10

You have the name right
if a little bit elliptical
on the side of the alphabet
      where meaning doubts
      the existence of rhyme
a lemon tree in our back yard
drops its fruit in winter
      theory makes story
      on this rain day
I don't know how to
   forget the loss of
   a way to summon
   the book
      (there is no
        way to summon
        the book —
just watch it come
      like your breath
      on the lake or
      my body erupts
with exit
      which way to go

Cardinal II

How did you fit
    such a large poem
into such a small space
                    or was it a
            painting that time,
    and did it fold paper
    from the creased point
    of *if*   to *is*
if so, where *is* the desire?
                    in a piano playing
                    blues with a
                    little tremble
        that shiver holding against
        crayons and litter and
            elegance, blasted
        the chickens and the eggs
    are safe,   petting plumes
    and looms there to give
    semblance to resemblance
    far or not far from

Dare He Hum

One wants to ask of love
   as
if there's a choice

it doesn't hurt to
   be
the one you want to know

when all else fails it
   can
rain on the tin roof

finally, no lack of
   decision
merits one's speech

some moments before the
   end
the light switch falters

we wanted only to
   fuck
in our own bed again

any language said, asked,
   gathers
itself toward disunion

ask or don't ask and you shall
  have
what you never anticipated

walk all the way around an
  island
until it becomes a continent

favored sounds compile sweet
  jam
on october night's losses

not just to
  kiss
but that also

to dance an airy step and not
  land
anywhere except

if I sometimes get
  mad
it's only stupid, only

over the waves and
  nary
a wet moment

where you don't sing
   only
not you the sharp note

if you want the intensity
   put
it there

why announce a
   question
when the tree moves

knowing no
   reason
to explain the slightest

don't kiss and leave to
   tell
time

as if it all adds
   up
this time unlike another

the shape of the mouth pronouncing
   vowel
is how you come to me

yes, that's it,
  what
did you say

you have probably breathed
  xenon
and much else

yes, that's it,
  what
did you say

more has passed than
  years
and more entered, through

we move away from
  zero
with light steps

IV

Pushing Water 9

thank you for the book
to write in to lie down in
to find place in   this place of phrases

(forty words of one syllable is
          this the american rhythm?)

thank you for the book

I moved the salt and pepper shakers around the table and moved
the truck around the streets and moved thread in and out of holes
in paper and moved my self in and out of rooms and nothing really
moved except the light a doctor just shined in my eye that feels
older than its partner, my other eye

                    green is in my world like

                              light and wind

Pushing Water 10

the rose is green   livid green
green when you shall no more speak
                 the green and
           dovegrey countries of
              the mind

Love that is a stone endlessly in flight
unless there is / a new mind there cannot
be a new / line

leap awake and see green
                 or sea green around
                 the cape the point
                 the push La Push
                 and its smoking salmon
and Butt's
Café where gather
from the rain people
from here and everywhere
they come
by the water

                     a new line

the layout like a city
             this city dispersed to
                 desert on the edges
                 desert at the center
it's a green desert
                 means a pause
                 in the center
       a dry heat
                 beats the dust in the air
and leaves thought
       to fly away

dust   lost   cost
what most love
brings home brings
away from home
(the beautiful thing)
            dances in a room
            where the railroad goes
            by and screams of commerce
and she moves in air

                        in air moves

  the air

                (italicized phrases from William Carlos Williams)

Pushing Water II

put paint on paper
and paint on paint
rub with fingers and
heel of hand and scratch
until a light inhabits
the color, there with
color and behind green
and blue

                I don't know how
you do that, love,
you
place the light

exactly there
not the beginning
but made and
before the beginning
permission, return
the color no longer
paint but light

      some men took a printing
press onto a frozen lake
and printed a book and
that's all the book means

                some one else made
                a small book and
                it became an ear
ring a set of
ear rings

      some one made a book
shaped like legs another
made a book bound with
a shower cap

Pushing Water 12

                                        certain slants
                                        on winter days
                                        light or summer
                                        fall on without
                                                    respite
                                        certain words
            slant   and recombine

from the air on one side
                            an echo the language
                            repeats itself
repeats itself

and the dirt on one side
to walk with no shoes
and glass and tar and

word and echo
word and silence

air is cut with motion
                            trapeze in motion
as though grace
could save a language
in the dirt on the
other side of air

what syllable falls here

            flight combs the language into
                        raw sound of free voice
will water fall and edge
            fall away from air
pushing water   air and   light

pushing water

Pushing Water 13

not the rhyme but the measure
        my measure lies in bed
        and waits

and after that   after night
        on a swing in a park
        smelling of cherries
            ripe and untouched
other than the need to talk
        the need to taste

        Not only a few mornings ago
        but from the tower years ago
        I gained speech from your
        willingness to embrace and
        sing   there, sound flies
        speech lies and rises
            let go   let go
        the water breaks

back yard carnivals grab
        heat and factual wetness
        of this summer's place wet
place of living
        take off clothes and
        stand with fan blowing

        memory of flying through
        air pushing cold water
        at hot
entrance

Pushing Water 14

one sister says to the other,
"my handwriting isn't better
than yours, just more
readable"   and later, reporting
what she said to a boy, 11 years
old, "I can kick just as well
in a dress as in pants"

                    thank you for the book
                    I said, and your
                    place in it somewhere
near the salt and pepper
and the act
of diving into water
he came back to the surface
and breathed
I always bring water
        to the table and place
it before you
        the whole of the work is
the sound of the work
is the structure of

            breaks   to the surface   breathes

        the dream   :
I walk into one sister's
room, to offer counsel.
when leaving, I see the other
in a corner by the door
with a baseball bat.   she swings
the bat with all her strength
across my shins.
I wake, screaming, crying /
                    as Williams said, the best
thing a man can do for

his son, after he is
born, is to die
and what about a daughter?
does she thrive from death
push herself
into the water without
checking for cold

come out of the corner
swinging?   where are the knots

one must untie?

Pushing Water 15

some precepts:
       don't mix symmetrical
              typography with asymmetrical typography
       don'tt set
              type vertically, nothing ever
              looks correctly aligned, as
              each letter has its own
              width
       try always to avoid
              borders and boxes
              because appropriate layout
              and spacing can do the
              same work without
              the fuss
       and as to fuss, decoration
              qua decoration
       is usually pretty boring
unless decoration is the message
                          and more
                    the watchword
       let small markers that occupy a
       small part of x-height and don't
       create a visual block lie
       outside the justification, they
       cause less visual noise that
       way   apostrophe or quotation
              I was taught
              never to set 8 point type
              unleaded, but then
              it just looked right that
              way, there are
       no rules not to break when
                    the need calls, in that way
       much like punctuation
                      grammar
              and etiquette

Duncan wrote,   on the top
of the page he returned to
me, newsprint page on which
stood *Passages: In Blood's Domaine,*
          "something more than a
          pleasure to see
                    that my notation can
                    be translated into a typography"

                    blue and black and red

          condensery of color and
                              metal alphabet with numbers
                              and marks of all kind
                    made to be the total
                              articulation of the sound
                              of the poem   made
                    in this condensery out of
                              grocery lists and children
                              sleeping and
          dancing in front of windows
                              in a downtown
                              bar to nothing but
                    a driven beat
while down the
          block the auctioneer asks who
                              will pay 100   200   300
                              800 for color rubbed
                              to light or poem
                              made of letters made
                              of a few precepts   no
                              ideas but in things only
                              emotion endures   the poem
                              must at all points
                                        disperse

Cardinal 12

only comes into
        tree fallen,
                pavement gap,
        articulate rain
        if not silence
   in the face
        fact or alteration —
conscious, convivial, contention of
   made place for children
                in the book
        never closed
ask what constitutes
space between *not the book*
and *the book,* grand
        collage in the making
        never *un*tuned
             when loss
        acts as savior
  fence
        falls to water

Cardinal 13

made a line
    twelve small girls in a row
    who begin to
        step and
        fall to a point
begin means break
        and more than two globes
joined at center to form
        disjointed heart
            that moves west
                finds home
        mad and happy
            dance for the
    syllable turns sound
        to consonance
never consolation or
            solace, find
        a place to read what
    moves inside and outside
        the lines

Pushing Water 16

from the tragic foot   the variable foot
                    the left foot leads
                    and dance is duration
                              how long the tone lasts
               and what can be said within
                    its continuance   (your mouth
                                             at my hips)

everyone has left the room
          two in a bed and
                    the youngest a sofa bed
                              in a room lit through
                                        an edge of glass
                    between dream and night
                    I walked
                                        across blocks and ravine
                                        to a window where
               she met me, we were fourteen, not
                              knowing what or where to do
                                        what we wanted only

               the air
               pushes water from one to the other

Pushing Water 17

some precepts for morning and children

one and one half cups flour
preferably half whole wheat
and half unbleached white
but health and taste
may substitute one
fourth cup corn meal for
flour, if corn meal is
used, add two teaspoons
sugar or a little less,
measure by hand not
by spoon, into flour
mix two teaspoons
baking powder a half teaspoon
salt and a good sprinkle
cinnamon

in another smaller bowl beat
two eggs slightly add one
and one half cup milk, two
tablespoons vegetable oil or
melted butter and a few
drops of lemon extract, stir
all these together well then
stir them into the flour
mix, on a griddle heated
to medium (drops of water
will skitter away)
there) (add no oil to griddle
if it has a non-stick surface otherwise
perhaps rub a little oil on it with
a paper towel and be careful
not to burn your hand) drop
about one third cup of this
batter, flip over when

bubbles are on top and edges
glisten and look solid, cook
only about a half minute on
the second side, put butter
and syrup or whatever you
desire (could be yogurt and
berries, or butter cinnamon and
sugar or what you will)
on one or more of these
and give to your children and
when they are four or five years
old teach them to make this breakfast
with you

if there are enough share
one or more with your lover
and remember to post the recipe
on your refrigerator so others
can see and copy it

Pushing Water 18

from Halfdane at Hrothgar
      to melancholy Dane awash
in what dreams may come
            neither valor nor death
                but the space between
                first sensory apprehension
                    and perception between
                perception and thought
                      space never
                discovered though charted
                    chemically through
          nervous systems shared
                    before language games
                gaps in cognitive science
          leave more than Horatio
                    dreamed in his philosophy
      we are only half   the other
          half may not be retrieved
                from watchhouse point or
                    in the patterns *uttered when*
                    I speak and *I speaks*
stunned and signed by wits beside oneself is an address
                1243 or 2833 or 5020
                we are numbered next
                door to a dog named Charlie
                or down the alley from
                four blonde boys playing basketball
                two architects continuously re-
                creating a dwelling place a
                young actress's younger sister
                in an upstairs room making
                love to her young boyfriend
                casting shadows on a window

shade these communities of form define
at least some of our steps

dance steps with pots crashing
of language

gather and disperse contract
and release
pushed one against another

Pushing Water 19

she never said   my mother that is
       that a false statement
       was a *lie*   instead she
       called it
       a story   and *don't tell*
       stories   meant *tell no*
       lies

I think this has   colored my view of fiction except that
everything becomes fiction when *true story* is an oxymoron

tell the truth but tell it slant
         means to allow
             a little of the light in
to the place of the telling
        and certain slants are ways
            of walking toward either
story or truth as much
as one becomes the other
in the wave on the beach
where glass grinds smooth
retains color and awaits
       the slanted push of
          uncertain waters

what time is it?
four ninety eight to seven
under the cowboy moon
what day is it?

      aren't you here and
is the sun shining what
kind of report are you making?

what happened?
       that was another time

and if you survived and
still breathe, that's enough
to know
the transition from ear to oar
        here to how was the dinner that
makes peace in a turning
phrase
        black night fell and
guests found, alone
or in pairs, place to
rest until the black
raven cried
and once again
the tide changed

Cardinal 14

because asked for
   time of day and
   rhymes other world
       of inside out
       a pout of rounding
            anywhere from doe
       to mar, a spot
on history, who so
       list to hunt
   I know, I know
it's an old hat
worn in a time of
recompense, reconnoiter
rely on someone else's
       instincts for what's left
        of the day, light
  holds out for more
          just when a visitor
       asks that time
       turn it over, again

Pushing Water 20

the house of art has white walls
with writing on them,   the house of art's sister is
blue   how are you?

to arrive is to end so why
not keep going down the hall
or in the painting of the
Gunnison River gorge a young girl pointed out pink
sky beyond the gentle ledge
where the artist must have
stood

the lens distorts as soon as
I sees, against its will
it retreats to a seat by
the mirror, where only
what precedes us in the
room comes into view
deep room with narrowing
white walls, without

cracks, stainless
steel chairs hold bodies in trust
to sleep, or wake

nothing wants to move
(inertia)
                stir the heat
pretend the ice moves slowly
down the back up
the other side between
the breasts

Suspend

over ocean / air dance / passing body

           a wing and a word

over, the water

           or out

looms and comes

       and there,

           two birds

no message

       say

       syllable and

           counting to seven

           four and thirty

                       times or time

                       upon a shelf

                making store

                       grain of wood in

             stead, stay

           these muscles

         in groups

     mold response, seeing

          in an octopus eye

              one's own

                       mobility

                    birch by the sea
                              square, curious
glass, rock, wood, sand
          materials in which
                    losses
          for the walking
                    voice takes
                    fear out of time
          state the obverse
                    fly

in a line or and

                              as these things come
                    fruit on a tree plucked
                              of leaves
today gone again

for a word

                    a way

                    trapeze here
                              and robes, caught
          or undone
                    children in circles, run
                              to light
                    a bit, an ort, a way above
                              where light goes

two on a bar over
            space, only
more than,
            count again, this step
    in, above, from
            and more than any except
                    light again

    prayer, she
            said, the thing
                    the in between or
        among and what
                    is not there at all
        leaf away, here

    square making
            star each morning
    strings move and ear
                    awake again
        water out window
falls to some
            ground once and
                    leg moves
        out

strain to not strain
    eye above for
        trapeze float
           or flow
      on no surface
         reflection for
         light, also finds

        never enough rain
          so pipes and
          tubes matter
             this way
              of flying to
                 dry air

      around and about
the house

    farther and father
           strand, here and
           distance
        the desire to go
           through waves
              and where
             exactly

a leaf and a lake
ten and turn
to work and walk
observe the changes
hear language
inside out
where one syllable
comes to another
tending

comes to one
to morrow
light, heat, pass
and
move eyes
this going
ache wants
austere
fruit for a lesson

green wood or dry
as air in,
hearing just
beyond tuning
creek turns, a fish
still there, kept and
returned,
barely
moving

green

green

green

going

gray

green

green

green

gone

gift

green

there

not what is not

said

but everything

that is not the

case

air moving now

slow and upon all

parts of skin

all there is

to know

                              stars in the lens
                                        not distance
                         as such, collapsed
                    from looking through
                              as though light,
                    years, disappear
                              up a road to
                                        observe what
                    can't
                              answer

                         points going
                                   every where
               graphing the world
                                   this enters light,
               order

               center of flower
                         yellow-
                                   green dot
               outer
                         moving pink
                                   from pale
                         to rose
               of

just a flash
      and a flurry
what happened?
      was something here?
         white and blue and
      past, passed

Pushing Water 21 (Meryle Alexander 1918-)

I

there can
or can
can
there

some
way
some way

gone and
gone

"so terrible"
she said
"to grow old"
so
will she
forget
the oxygen
or the pills
today?
tomorrow?

from where I stand
there is no
no
no

not to stop
breathing
or stop
breathing

2

let's not pretend
she never did
and never
tried to make us
be anything for
her and
never hid any
thing or put on
a little girl
voice she was
strong enough
for what came
and more and for
never which is
where she's going and
she knows it so
we should too with
no blinders and no
pretending no blood
on our eyes no
false smiles
it isn't pretty even
though I think she's
going to join
the atoms of
earth and blood
let's not pretend
she's going anywhere
we haven't been it's
just that we don't
know and we can
not know yes
we can *not*   let's

go there with
her and with our
hands
open

3

turn one half turn
with a key to
open the oxygen
flow
put the small green plastic
funnel over the clear
funnel that's inside
the round plastic
piece and attach
the top plastic
piece by screwing
it on and squeeze
the drops of medicine in
to the open top and
attach the tube at bottom
that connects to the
machine and attach
the breathing tube at top
and press the on
switch

Cardinal 15

for Hannah Weiner

will you carry a light
daughter pail
the cabinet the sink oh
Hannah
now which book your visions
passed on
I have no long guns
I will carry a light
revolving door
and close it open for the night
the letters are BIG
enough to walk in
       dreamed of rollerskating
       into Manhattan
do you really want the desert
       in your ear
at the end of the table we
       don't say now
SPOKE
       and it's again

Cardinal 16

                 green
         green
green
         going
             gray
                     green
         green
             green
gone
                    gift
         green
             there,   said

         *   *   *
                          points going
             every *where*
graphing the world
                   this enters
         that point of
order, light

v

Pushing Water 22

a speech

in the center
of the page

sweet
thought

another one
and fine

find

speech

center

maybe not

*   *   *

abloo

        ramboff
farrarra

alfontinese
peralmibatodo defensimobb righteelee

oofoom

        fleeaplomb

ratherimplone

abloo
too
abloom

*   *   *

arise
and
all

rise

right

awry

airy

are we?

*   *   *

ash to
can

tibulation   taboo

112

tar around

try   hard
try   on
       tired of onions

          as in
          can you

   caroon
          tune

*   *   *

          bent toward
          a knee

annie

   frank as a bee
      fresh

          from growing
to unbend
      unbind
            page one

*   *   *

clomp

around a while

a romp

rumptuous

romance

or morass

don't touch it

file it away

where

there

undone

*   *   *

a cluster
a toaster

a roast
a coast

a round
the ground

a name
an aim

a said
aside

east
above

or down where the crumbs

the birds

*   *   *

I suppose

                          quite serious

            should be miserable

curves of a white lily

cool ivory

        ears and eyes

                who it was

*   *   *

     double back
        and front forward

perceived as winged

            or capable

                culpable

       come on

           where ya goin'

                could be the wind

                could be the rain

      or a bone out of place

          a bone place

               beautiful and

                   specific

*   *   *

leap   and
           let
           stay

go   go   go
                    far in
                    to the turn
                    the twist
                    the thrust
                    and toss
                    and leap
                              shot out
                              put there

*   *   *

let us fix tomorrow
          not upon
                    far windows
along the side

                    a tree structure
          or syllable

                    wanting
                    wanting

          nothing

waiting

lead us not

*　　　*　　　*

linkable as in
　　　sales of goods
　　　　　　sailing gone
　　　　　　for good

　　　　　　for air
　　　　　　for water

　　lean on it

　　　　　　as in here
　　　　　　　　　　or no
　　　　　　where

*　　　*　　　*

not to make anything

not to do anything

not to want anything

*   *   *

tarry there   subtle
          fluid   strange
                    perfume

          pert   tune

                    inopportune

grace and
                    dim woodland

          where it could be said

                    the mere shapes and patterns
                              of things
          stoutness
                                        adore her
                    public and private life

*   *   *

the words
          the wily
          woods
          woo
               oo

118

why did you
say what you
did say, did
you say it?

                              another day
                              in the woods

with an alphabet

*   *   *

why not
        not to
                              atone
        tune the
        piano
                arpeggio air

VI

Pushing Water 23

for Jackson Mac Low

lamp light
bulb light
sun light through window
airport light
airplane lights   through window
flashing lights   through window
where light   through
when light   after
why lightthis
after light

designation of light
remembrance of light
creation of light

the movement of light through a prism

the half eternity
move occurs Voices each make eye ninety-three the
other form
light inwardness glass hole transformed
twinned hemispheres retina One unlinks glass head
and
periphery reversing in snails moment

yellow highway lights all in a row
neon lights seen from an airplane

in one order the lights in another order the lights

the movement of light through a prism

the hinged Euridice

metanoia of void eardrum may early nothing their
own first
lyre its glass held through
the happen Reality once under glass holocaust
a
proportion ringed in swirled merely

light of the eaten moon
protected in lines escaped
from the church steeple apex
where geometric light imagined

tissue-thin monotone
light undisturbed
by colors

the movement of light through a prism

the heave expands
moves of *voions espesse* Matrix energy number to
of *fathomed*
live in got him the
throat him rid of us grassblade he
at
preaching rustling in sun mountain

while in lemon light
I am my self
a complex of light   insufferable

the movement of light through a prism

the hearing explained
magnified obliquely visible existence man equilateral not that

One falls
a lake in green half through
turtle Head reply O upon grave him
angels
perpetual rose it shall morning

light through red maple leaf
plucked from the tree just
before fallingl

fallen light
dry light
halcyon light
among of goes green light

the movement of light through a prism

to transform ear
mind of voice ends morning every noise through
on foot
let it grass heart trust
the hail root O unto ground how
a
place rock in sown mad

blackboard the porch of old house on pickard avenue

CRAZY WISDOM
FORGET THE QUESTION
FORGET THE ANSWER

shimmer path *Hero* paradise light of the street with leaves air floating
dance among above and below the arch of late fall trees time extending
self in sublime act embrace
(Norman, Oklahoma, December 12 2004)

head warming light in still air ten minutes later
                                same street other world

the movement of light through a prism

throughout hand ever
moved out void eye mower eyes nature that
of fleshliness
lit intensest glass Her The
To how ray out Unconscious gleaming his
and
prepared return is sheathed *Millenium*

grayish American light in a room of books at 42 North Moore street
leads to clear low light in a room of bright banging music
before light of thirty western bran flake days
and blue jaundice healing a future giving light
and microlens light through light seen from the observatory on
Dmitri's mountain

all part of the same light

the movement of light through a prism

turns hills each
Murmurer overspills very earths Man equilateral *No the*
of fractured
lost is Gold hive taps
to head resonant of *un grottoes* here
and
Pool return its symmetry *mirage*

all part of the same light

indigo
light over vicissitude electrons

toes open
far under crazy kisses
marine yearnings
gitanjali iridescent red light

bloomsday light

french sonnet light

missing the light

beyond the light

Pushing Water 24

for Robert Creeley

I am coming I
am always coming
am sometimes there
and here   here
you are   all the you
is where here is

there *is* a story
the words *are* given
the woods thick and deep

the desert wide   alive

the wise surprised   all
going coming begun undone

This is the place and
were I to deny the
fact of it   where
then am I   I
am coming I
am

the leaves have fallen
and sun warms
a world in which

will you come with
me

* *

Curious this
being in the world

eating   writing   as
if being watched

* *

if you
went out into a
field and hid
there

by

what is going

by

what is going

by

what is

                    going

Pushing Water 25: *Astrobiology as Perfume*

Forty-two or 42
976 and/or
       "billions and billions"
this is the five-year mission
                (don't panic)
     here is your towel
inside an atom is a word

           stay tuned for a late encounter
           with Baruch Spinoza
                Behind The Music
     meanwhile   *A*
               round of fiddles playing Bach
        pronounce it: a (ay)
        pronounce it: a (æ)
        pronounce it: a (uh)

It is most liberating to admit —
I don't know where I am
        green streaks in the sky
        blue light in a hospital room

   begin again
   to undo
   the beginning
       fudge
       not fugue
       foster the fester
       test the toast
       toss the salad

why have I come here?
        should my pants be tighter?
   star within star
   or so it looks
        microlensed on Dmitri Sassalov's
        birthday on Mt. Hopkins 1997

two girls want to look into the telescope
but no one does
the telescope aimed by computer
and commanded to generate image maps
on a screen
and this is how we see a star within
        a star lens
                    the world is made of mustard
                    and we move slowly in it
                    the moon is made of custard
                    and we can't taste it
        Spectra of the night unite!
                        write me a letter
                        sing me a song
        Oh Mona where are your southern
        charms now, you call to my top
        head, fall on our ears and
        listen with,
        to, the other
                    swing low, park swing
                    cherries and artichokes
                    berries and pomegranates
                            this is the way the world sings
                            this is the way the world sings
                                    not with a bang
                                    but with a big bang
        for every atom there is (as good belongs to you)
                    an equal and undiscoverable
                    contradiction

                        whenever I speak I
                        speaks
                    whoever eye hears
                            ear hands
                            let go   let go
        but no one was holding on
                    ever or

in the first place or
after the afterblast

(this is a blue examination book
Are you being examined?
   what does it feel like
   between your legs and
   behind your arms and
   in the back of your head?)

once a wall was knocked down
and there before the knocking
was a mural — Shakespeare and
a globe — and on the other
side, Samuel
Johnson and a dictionary

   Is that the beginning point?
     when all hell breaks loose?

       dunno dunno dunno
     dull now down north do not

   every syllable births a syllable
   every knot ties a knot
   word = road = door

peel the glass darkly
        pearl of modest price

              I am the inkman
              you are the inkman
              we are us
                 (panic)
                 eleven
                 one by one

Cardinal 17

as cost to counter —
        what eye casts
                and asks
                hand to go
chart patterns of
                three and two
                either trace
                or make
holes and thread plots
        place for language
                (to lead or
                follow)
        go from there
        to anywhere forms
                translation
meet at the corners
        where any sound
knows its edge
again

Cardinal 18

for Gil Ott

flying Tatlin's glider
or a paper horse
            through singing air
into the public domain
            where moon
            (it doesn't run
            on gasoline)
filled with whole notation
finds where history
                        has left us
(it has left us)
                        or is there dissent
                        in the stone, where
                        the book imposes

as if air as if song
            and a space between one
            group of words and another
to lie down among

VII

Pushing Water 26

a wind blows now to then
or catch a wave and fly

how many ways of pushing water
how many times of pushing water
how many years of pushing water

as a child a memory was false
of walking in a yard hand outstretched
after a butterfly that landed on the palm
not butterfly but bee suddenly

as a child a memory was false
of a hand outstretched a palm again
walking forward with a palm
a palm set fire to

pushing water here to there
wash away the bee
soothe the sting
dampen the fire
soothe the burn

the present pushes water into the past
blows a wind now to then
catches a wave and flies

the present pushes into the past
the present pushes water into the past
the present pushes into the past

memories are dreams
memories have subsided
dreams have subsided
water remains
water and the pushing
wind and the wave and the flying

the present is part memory part dream part
pushing water and wind into the past and finding
water pushing back

nature is a story we tell ourselves
not the spots of time that sustain time
not red in tooth and claw
not a whore
not a note not a not
not the stories we tell ourselves
and only the stories we tell ourselves
that can be false and still require water
to put them out to soothe to remember

water flows pushes moves stops somewhere never the same twice river
ocean

water   pushes

water

pushes

Pushing Water 27

and only the stories we tell ourselves

and spots of time pushing water

oh there is blessing in this gentle breeze
                a gentle friend in early years assists
                change from place to place and mind to mind
                pretend identities a game unwinding
                with words, in later years
                a friend believes in word sparks
                sparks fly from words in rituals
                old and newly made wherein
                a life in words reveals itself
                in rhythms bop bop beyond where
                singer sleeps to slender singer

the ghostly language of the ancient earth
                the frothy language of the creek behind
                the house of the gentle friend behind
                the house of the friend with the horse
                from which flown to the earth for fear
                of speed through the trees near the creek
                that ends in a pond with a rumor of one
                old catfish denizen of ancient earth
                and new dreams of children almost
                no longer children there in the green
                in the wet in the speed in the dream

from street to street with loose and careless heart
> in a foreign land where street and path
> wander through small hills and valleys
> where *mizu* and *scoshi* are the only known
> words, water and small and no sense of
> pushing water, but in the small moments
> everything is pushing two languages
> one like wind hill to hill grass earth
> of path unknown always lost not lost the moment
> present even now when words have given way
> to spots of water

had lain awake, on breezy nights, to watch
> moon rise on Pacific Ocean south of Half
> Moon Bay having climbed down a hillside
> to reach a beach of drift tides and sand where
> an old quilt made by grandmother in the small
> town of Burns Flat Oklahoma served its last duties
> as bed on that sand free of study and worry far
> distance short time from childhood when first
> the exhaustions of sheer distance set in not
> yet as exhaustions but propulsions through
> reddish, purplish, small things glazed with rain

abject, depress'd, forlorn, disconsolate
> arranged, designed, forgotten, disturbed
> alone destined forsaken dashed
> these were days of finding no self to echo self
> or when found, strains of clarinet called her
> or mountain wanderings once shared in snow
> at thin air heights where slip and slide stops
> in a blue tent in that space where ground
> and sky give way to one another her call
> to remain in the mountains and play
> for others mouth to reed to star to snow

to part from company and take this book
> take this book to the air
> to the water
> to the bicycle
> stolen behind the home of the one
> who brought the person to the book
> and stole hearts and thoughts beyond
> the book or the person not lost in
> buttons and islands of cast off power
> no the casting off is place for first
> venture, love's wandering

five years are vanish'd since I first pour'd out
> or twenty-nine years since first step
> mis-step, no not mis-step, but step
> that leads to turn, turn to book
> on landing over water, turn to
> women in trouble leading to
> thin love, not love but time lost
> days and years for love's winter
> wandering ventures away from
> itself away from everything
> that matters into water

they move about upon the soft green field
> they move about amid the soft green
> and yellow sunflowers they are three
> and two are those of home those of
> love's second venture north after
> first wanderings in the actual desert
> a space with saguaro
> and rock and paintings on rock
> paper and canvas this is
> the resolution this the revolution this the
> turning that does not stop turning, pushing

as oftentimes a river, it might seem

> the first shock of the river that runs without
> water causes memory to return to a fountain
> of water pours over an edge of stone
> a sheet of water one might push a hand through
> push a word through sheets of water like sheets
> of sound and water fresh
> in a pool below a stone tower
> where moon outside the window welcomed
> by words written on wood good day good night
> good dream and life in water

to the last punctual spot of their despair

> spot of mud adobe home where birth
> occurs on day of stolen car found not
> drivable a gentle friend arrives
> with bicycle offers help and when help
> comes it comes from a sister
> moving from home to room of late
> night screams of welcome into wet world
> of light and spot of time that pushes into
> all past and present and times to come
> the call of daughter life of the dream

until that natural graciousness of mind

> a state that never remains more than
> a moment, or group of moments continue
> or collapse, space is central fact
> but space exists with time
> and neither without witness, the act,
> the person, generosity of witness the
> generosity of witness, for love you are
> the color and you give the color and you
> witness the color and that first call first
> dream remains grace and through grace

I love a public road: few sights there are
                    public begins with two and we are
                    public whether speaking words in groups of
                    two or two hundred or hanging paintings where
                    people walk and mingle and say words
                    and words for pictures are the beginnings
                    of words and words are the beginnings of pictures
                    amid words and pictures another daughter calls
                    and comes and says hello and speaks of animals
                    and numbers and after two months a northern trip
                    and snow in winter and raspberries in summer

by reason and by truth; what we have loved
                    Basho says that only half or slightly
                    more than half of the subject of the poem should
                    be revealed but the whole subject is in the act
                    of pushing water as past pushes to now and now
                    pushes to past and the whole subject is the meaning
                    of living in time and not in time at all as we know
                    and love from day to day but as we know
                    nothing ever leaves and nothing begins except
                    at all points gathers and disperses
                    until final water all or nothing is contained

                              italicized lines are consecutively from each
                                   of the thirteen books of the 1805
                                   edition of Wordsworth's The Prelude

Pushing Water 28

there it is   the quivering of lines
     the queering of lines   the leering of lines
the looking of lines   the final or
     ongoing inconsistency of light
         water   wind

     brushy along the surface of the water
     growing more delicate
         thinner   paler
  this way and that in all directions

         ways of coming in
    brush strokes   hand liftings
age's gaze   chest rise

    how does need come into the poem

    she found the raspberries along the fence

    found   along

Pushing Water 29

What is the structure of a leaf?
What is the consistency of a cell?
How can they be suspended in air?
How might a word or group of words be like a leaf, falling?
Is air required?
How does need enter the poem?
Is it the quiver in a line?
Is it the cry in the tone?
Can it be what has been left out?
If one writes, what and where is two?

Can isolation embrace community?
Is it all language?
Can color find sound?
Why continue when the rain falls?
Who wrote the final syllable?
Can a sound be repeated?
How far can one drive a letter without becoming wet?
Must an echo have a precedent?
How do we determine the speed of a consonant?
What is the place of appetite in poetic space?

Should this arrangement of questions be structured in terms of the
        repetition of the first few words, i.e. "Is it" followed by "How
        does" or "How do" followed by "What is the?"
Does structure matter?
Is matter structured?
If the frame experiences an injury, is the content of the frame also hurt?
How much hurt is required?
To what extent is hurt chosen?
What is your name?
On what kind of surface did you take your first step?
Have you heard the space between blue and white in a painting?
How far does a letter stretch?

What is in the box?
How can I address the rock in the field?
Does "by hand" mean the same thing as "from the heart"?
Are five holes better than four?
Who determined the pitch of middle "C"?
Have you forgotten?
Can the feel of a knotty word in the mouth taste sweet?
Is a pun only a pun if intended as a pun?
Can a person join a sentence?
Have you held your breath in a moment's green and piney syllable?

What does one man turning turn to?
Did she play the concerto or return to the aviary?
Have you pushed water until a missile flew?
Can I understand why light might heal a child?
Where is the hole?
Where is the other glass of whiskey?
Does altitude matter to a letter ascending?
If the descent beckons, must the ascent have beckoned?
Why balance the book?
Why are there ten in each?

Is everything flawed?
What about the dress?
Do I fit?
Am I fit enough?
What if the size of the needle is too big to fit into the hole in the fold
of the pages?
From what point of view can one tell whether the hummingbird has
        arrived at the window?
Can gender be propulsive or militaristic?
Why would she disperse the sections of the poem, letting them fly into
        one another?
Is it enough to want to see the point?
Why not just tell them?

When you saw the coyote on the side of the street were you afraid for it?
What is the exact midpoint of the journey through the page?
Is it sharp?
Can a point be squashed or expanded or stretched to become a field or
        a war?
Who went down to the ships?
Can a fiddle be round and still play?
If I quit, did I lose?
What kind of profit motive would cause you to question the dream?
If cold can there be a blue hat?
Why did you leave?

When she wrote her life why didn't she leave it alone?
Is there a language that can not be translated unless waiting is
required?
Does darkness have a focal point?
Who loves what remains?
How hard is jade?
How hard is the test?
How did you find the new location where you settled after a move to
        begin a new story?
What gives?
What recompense is enough to make you feel good about giving all
        you have gained?
How fast can you drive with a mask on?

Where is your mother?
When does one become old enough?
When the oxygen is flowing through the tubes and through the nose
        and into the lungs, are there specific points of feeling along
        the way?
Does a question go away?
Why are her feet always cold?
Will she outlive the year?

Can an inquiry about money be turned from a personal challenge into
    a joyful sound?
Have we now gone indoors to stay?
Are the steps real or metaphorical?
Where have we gone or where have I gone and which is correct?

Are there ten left or only nine and does the present allow itself to be a
    border between then and when?
At what point does now become a political question?
Is this random?
What would you rather forget, a meal or a mouth?
When faced with an alternative can you poise between?
Why signify and why not signify?
Is there a point at which all doesn't fall apart?
Can you cry on demand?
Who is asking the questions?
Why do you want to know?

Pushing Water 30

what, two?   Watteau
       blue sky   green bowl
somewhere after the fact of language
      a field   a fold
               fluency
         or flow

to talk   relying on the necessity of
     a listener   would it be heard
in a forest   alone
         green above
           blue erased

a cluster   accuser   accursed
   black spot   ink or metaphor

strange turning man   the enormous
     tragedy of the dream   emerging
   from a sheet of water
        a wafer
           (to live)
to sustain talk over thirty years
      thirsty   135 days with
no measurable precipitation
     the javelina scavenge behind the house
       coyote near the schoolyard

no water to push   no wet pores
vapors   what pours   *(Watteau)*
    he came costumed as if in a painting

       where is the substance
         perhaps gone

     call me poet   call me near
       dip me in the water

not Watteau   or what two
                          or what gives
or what if?

                          water
relentless and to make   *water*
relentless be *let go*   *water*
to make push be *allow*
to make love be *forgive*
to make language be *anything but silence*
      and silence too

            we in the stream
            unplug our ears
            in the middle
            of the enormous tragedy

      weave in the dream
      applaud our fears
      inevitable
      until our most ragged
                          selves answer the question

            it's time again
                    green renewal springs
                    or minor repairs to the engine

      let us jump the hedgerows
                    (hardly hedgerows)
      let us be water

Pushing Water 31

rage on across the air
while witnesses stand
and photogenic girls stare

in the rain we run
with flattened hair
the bombing has begun

shame on us all for our fucking war
no one wins, we shame the whore
nothing is holy and all will die

shame on us for our fucking war
all is holy and all will die
the taste of lies

the taste in my mouth will not soon go
I sing lullaby with the tongue laid low
death is quick and death is slow

after the poem my daughter came
and asked for a lullaby —the poem ends and the lullaby begins
or the poem never ends, the war never ends, the lullaby never ends
the light goes into the air
the water goes into light and air
I ask my friends where the words end
the same answers
the same questions

in all the places I have been
the words have gone
they all are taken
the water pushes as far as it can

Cardinal 19

jewels glow and breathe out
as though stars go somewhere
                              else
headlands to desert to
streets with stone houses
all in all, black ink white paper
rubbed or printed
            where the lines
            bear or redeem
little but the organ's intent
to form a language
of us, our homes are yours as well
                              as well
it composes, blooms whether little
or much water recommends face
to face
            wash over the children
            in the light
            before it goes

Pushing Water 32

polis and   politicization
the way the word goes   away from the place that claims it
in error   claims it in error in order to place it
          in a confined space
to make it one
the way desire sounds
       verse   against or around
       to make against
       to make in spite of
       to make on its own
       to make the made thing that has a way of its own
       goes round   and round

       the word forced into a form that the social space allows
but to go against the social space the word must free itself
this may be too much

                              it is necessary
to construct not a social space for the making   but a multitude
of spaces for the multitude of the making
and the spaces that declare themselves   the space or the
better space
can be left alone   to collapse
into disunion
and out of disunion   words   that stop
somewhere